Legal Teams, Labor Unions, Negotiation, Record Keeping, and Employee Reviews

5 Organizational Behavior Books in 1

Louis Bevoc and Nicole Edinburgh

Published by
NutriNiche System LLC

Louis Bevoc books...simple explanations of complex subjects

Legal Teams	3
Labor Unions	15
Negotiation	31
Record Keeping	46
Employee Reviews	60

Legal Teams in Organizations
Their Roles and Value

Nicole Edinburgh and Louis Bevoc

Published by
NutriNiche System LLC

Louis Bevoc books...simple explanations of complex subjects

Introduction — 5
- Lawsuits — 5
- Contracts — 5
- Intellectual property — 5
- Employee Relations — 6

Assembly — 6
- Regulatory — 6
- Litigation — 7
- Employment — 7
- Corporate — 7

Objectives — 7
- Human capital — 7
- Projects — 8
- Security — 8
- Service — 8

Value — 9
- Return on Investment (ROI) — 10
- Circumstantial savings — 10

Managing — 11
- Appreciation — 11
- Workloads — 11
- Spending — 11
- Creativity — 11
- Knowledge — 12
- Style — 12
- Risk — 12

Improving — 12
- Limit diversification — 12
- Set clear goals — 13
- Educate clients — 13
- Establish think tanks — 13
- Outsource legal expertise — 13

Summary — 13

Introduction

Most organizations do not have internal legal teams due to the expense and justification. Lawyers typically do not work for low wages, so they need to add value to the organization in order to justify the wages they are paid. This means there needs to be some type of cost/benefit analysis before a legal team can be instituted.

One way to conduct a cost/benefit analysis is by looking at the cost of outside legal counsel. If this cost is going up year after year, then it might be time to explore an in-house team. Below are some of the more common reasons why outside legal costs go up for organizations.

Lawsuits - This is the most obvious reason for the average person. Lawsuits cost money….regardless of whether they are won or lost. They can drag on for years with attorneys continually getting paid for their services. Barring a retainer, hourly wages can easily be in excess of $500 per hour, and there is no guarantee of winning. Often times, the only guarantee is that the lawyer(s) will get paid.

Lawsuits also entail costs that are not as visible as the hourly wages charged by lawyers for their time spent working on the case. These expenses include charges for emails, faxes, memos, letters, and just about any other document that requires preparation. Cases that require any type of investigation also take on additional expenses. Then there are deposition fees, motions costs, and mediation charges that can be tacked on without notice. These expenses can add up to a large sum of money in a relatively short period of time and, worst of all, they can be incurred before the courtroom trial begins. Add to this the stress and anxiety that often accompany lawsuits and it is easy to understand why the cost of outside legal activities continually goes up for some organizations.

Contracts- Legal expertise is needed for companies involved in contract negotiations. For example, during real estate transactions attorneys are needed to look at contracts, offer advice on purchase options, clarify terminology, explain forms, act as an intermediary, and answer questions pertaining to legal aspects of the process. Sometimes specialized attorneys are necessary because they understand the laws in particular states or countries. These lawyers are available, but they are well-compensated for their services. If real estate deals become more common, then the amount of money spent on outside legal help increases…and there is little that can be done to prevent this increase because the outside expertise is necessary.

Similar to real estate transactions, attorneys need to review outsourcing contracts to look for potential problems. They examine clauses, terms, and conditions to be sure they are advantageous to the organizations that they represent. Since many companies are farming out work to focus on the aspects of the business that they do best, the costs for their outside attorneys are continually going up.

Intellectual property - Intellectual property is essentially something of value created by people's thinking. Many times this creation has no physical existence, such as a patented process, but others time it can be visually observed, such as a trademark on a product.

Examples of intellectual property include copyrights, trademarks, patents, and trade secrets. Books, music, names, and slogans can also be protected under intellectual property laws.

When organizations attempt to protect intellectual property, they need legal assistance because the process is technical and detailed. A patent, for example, can take years to get approved, and the costs do not stop until the process is complete. Worse yet, there is no guarantee that the patent will get approved, but the organization must still pay the costs associated with it. Over time, lawyer fees for intellectual property work can increase a point where they no longer seems justified...and that is when hiring an in-house legal staff turns into a reality.

Employee relations - Companies always have issues with employees that need to be resolved, and these issues increase as organizations grow and expand. Training, rules, regulations, policies, pay, and benefits are all examples of aspects of business where employee relations are important. Human resource personnel often handle much of the work that involves employee relations, but there is always the possibility of litigation if something goes wrong. For this reason, legal expertise is sometimes required, and the expenses associated with it can mount quickly.

In terms of employee relations, organizations with unions face greater legal challenges than those faced by non-union facilities. For example, lawyers are often present for management during labor negotiations. These attorneys try to get the best deal possible for the company, and sometimes this requires a lot of time and effort. Union facilities can see their legal fees increase drastically during contract negotiation years, and this is why some of them think about hiring an in-house legal team.

Now that you understand some of the reasons why outside legal costs go up for organizations, it is time to move on. The next section discusses the assembly of an in-house legal team.

Assembly

This refers to the make-up of the in-house team. In other words, the types of attorneys found on the team. The make-up varies based on the size of the organization and budget allotted for its development, but there needs to be a reference point so this book assumes the team is made up of five lawyers.

The head of the legal team is known as the director. This person reports directly to the CEO and is responsible for overseeing the activities of the other four team members. The other four members consist of a regulatory attorney, litigation attorney, employment attorney, and corporate attorney. Each of their roles and responsibilities is summarized below.

Regulatory – This lawyer makes sure all aspects of the business are in compliance with local, state, and federal regulations. He designs strategies for compliance and conducts the training required to implement and maintain those strategies. He works with other employees and, if necessary, outside counsel to ensure his effectiveness on the job. His goal is to minimize the risk of his company violating the regulations he oversees.

Litigation – This attorney specializes in lawsuits and lawsuit defense. She manages all phases of litigation from the initial investigation to the settlement. She works with witnesses, obtains documents, and conducts interviews in order to collect facts related to the case she is overseeing. She also handles the settlement negotiations after a verdict has been reached. Her goal is to minimize the risk of litigation for the company.

Employment – This lawyer handles all employment issues from hiring to firing and everything in between. She works with her employer to resolve disputes, establish wages and benefits, and terminate employees. She specializes in wrongful discharge and unemployment compensation because these are issues where risk needs to be minimized for the company.

Corporate – This attorney deals with corporate affairs including stock, hierarchal structure, organizational design, real estate transactions, and relationships with the community. He understands laws pertaining to contracts, taxes, securities, zoning, licensing, and intellectual property. He has more broad-based responsibility than any of the other lawyers on the team, and his goal is to minimize the risk of wrongdoing by the organization or its members.

Now you understand how an in-house legal team is assembled. The next section examines specific objectives of these teams.

Objectives

In-house legal teams are gaining momentum in terms of popularity with attorneys. Once thought of as last resort jobs, they are now considered a legitimate option by many lawyers…especially those who are recent graduates. In fact, some law schools are now offering courses geared toward practicing law in corporate environments. These courses train students on the important legal aspects of companies that need to be handled by in-house attorneys.

Since in-house legal teams are becoming more common, it is understandable that their usefulness is coming under closer scrutiny from the companies that employ them. Organizational leaders want to understand what they will get in return for an investment in their legal teams, and that understanding starts with an examination of the team's objectives. The following are some of the most important objectives of in-house legal counsel:

Human capital - Human capital refers to the knowledge and thought processes of employees' within organizations. It encompasses personality, social skills, creativity, innovativeness, and resourcefulness. In-house legal teams consider management of human capital an objective because they strive to draw from peoples' skills in order to make their organizations better. This often requires changing organizational structure or employee behavior in order to reduce risks involved. For example, a company wants to start manufacturing a new type of product that has to meet strict environmental regulations. The legal counsel needs to conduct research regarding the impact these regulations will have on the organization. Do employees have the knowledge to implement and maintain this product and its process? Will skilled employees need to be hired? Will employees leave the organization due to stress? These questions need to be answered before making a decision, and in-house counsel will lead the way.

Quite honestly, it could be argued that human capital management is an objective of all supervisors in organizations. However, difficult or crisis situations present challenges for most supervisors because they need to extract the best out of employees who are under duress. This requires persuasive oral skills, which are present in lawyers due to their education and training. Without proper management of employee knowledge and skills, companies can end up with major problems...and in-house legal teams are dedicated to minimizing the risk for those problems.

Projects - Project management is exactly what it says it is...the management of projects. Obviously, this is an oversimplified statement due to the variables involved, but it gives a general idea of the subject matter. Projects can last for hours, days, weeks, months, or years. In fact, some projects are never finished because they are not followed through to completion. However, regardless of the time involved, there needs to be people who oversee the process.

Many of the job tasks performed by in-house lawyers are project related. For example, a legal team is working on protecting a trademark of the company that employs them. This requires skilled expertise and can be quite complicated, but, in reality, it is simply a project that needs to be completed. Since attorneys are the primary employees working on this project, they need to manage it...and this makes project management an objective.

Security- Security refers to protection from external sources that seek to do some kind of harm. People are most familiar with security in terms of protection from other people who are hostile and trying to do some type of physical damage. However, in this book, security refers to protection of secrecy and protection from financial harm. Examples of secrecy are formulations, processes, and trademarks. Examples of financial harm are damage from lawsuits, theft of intellectual property, and degradation of image. The list of examples of secrecy and financial harm is quite extensive, but much of it centers on the protection of sensitive information.

Legal teams are exposed to a lot of sensitive information in organizations, and that information needs to be kept confidential and secure. Business decisions need to be made, but sensitive information cannot be divulged during the process. Fortunately, lawyers are trained in protecting the people they work for; thereby making the objective of security fairly easy to obtain.

Service - This is likely the most well-known objective of legal teams because they provide legal service for organizations. They replace outside counsel for most legal issues and, when outside attorneys are hired, the in-house team works with them to accomplish goals and objectives.

An example of service provided by attorneys is their management of company/government relationships. They work with various government agencies to help their organizations meet mandated requirements and conform to rules and regulations. This requires them to manage people and processes using their knowledge and abilities. They have high levels of direct contact with government officials; thereby requiring them to have a combination of experience and people skills. Without a doubt, the management of interaction with government agencies is a service needed by most organizations.

Another example of service provided by in-house legal teams is reporting. These teams are trained to document everything which results in them compiling a wealth of information. That information is used to create reports which are given to the appropriate personnel. For example, a report discussing a discrimination lawsuit filed by an employee is shared with the human resource manager because this information can be used to prevent future lawsuits. However, other reports generated by in-house counsel contain sensitive information that can only be given to top-level employees. For example, a report detailing profitability and executive expenses in a private corporation is only shared with the CEO. The CEO then decides who else will have access to this information because it is confidential.

The last example of service provided by in-house legal teams involves determining the risks involved in business transactions. Real estate purchases, rules, regulations, government interaction, charitable contributions, wages and benefits, and community involvement are all analyzed for risks. This information can then be used to determine if the risk needs to be mitigated. For example, attorneys at an oil company need to determine the risk involved with drilling for oil in a pristine area of Montana. The company owns the drilling rights to this properly, but the timing might be wrong due to a growing population of opposing environmentalists in the area. There could be protests that cause damage to the company's image or reputation, so the drilling project requires research before it begins.

Now you understand some major objectives of in-house counsel. Let's move on to an examination of the worth of these lawyers by showing how the value of in-house legal teams is determined.

Value

The roles of in-house legal teams differ based on the organization that employs them. For example, lawyers at advertising agencies might spend most of their time protecting intellectual property while attorneys at real estate offices spend most of their time reviewing contracts. However, regardless of the type of business, in-house lawyers always have the responsibly of examining the risks of business activities so decisions can be made. When risk is minimized and goals are accomplished, then the attorneys prove to their employer that they have value. If this value increases over time, then more funding is designated for the legal department. However, if this value decreases over time, then the legal department is scrutinized and possibly even eliminated.

So, what exactly defines value? That is a good question because all organizations are not the same. However, one common way that in-house attorneys add value is by breaking down legal documentation so it can be understood by middle management employees. Middle managers are involved in day-to-day operations, and their comprehension of the legal subject matter is critical for the understanding of the rank-and-file employees who perform most of the daily tasks. Most people who have worked in business are aware that an understanding of their job requirements is important for job performance. Without this understanding, it is difficult to accomplish organizational goals and objectives.

Another measure of the value of in-house legal teams involves tracking the amount of money saved by their services. Obviously, there is a cost for these lawyers, but there is also a payback when they perform optimally. That payback can be measured monetarily by evaluating the return on investment (ROI) and circumstantial savings as follows:

Return on Investment (ROI) - A simple way of thinking about ROI is that is measures the return of money after it is invested in some type of resource. In this book, that resource is a legal team. A high ROI shows that the investment was good because it returned more than it cost, and the opposite is true for a low ROI.

Organizational leaders have traditionally used ROI to measure investments made in their organizations. This makes good business sense, but it not entirely accurate when it comes to legal team investments. Legal teams need some type of benchmarking to be part of their ROI due to the types of problems handled and the internal restructuring that often takes place over time. ROI can be good one year and bad the next due to varying expenses, but those expenses might be justified by taking a closer look at the situation. For example, the settlement of a victorious lawsuit might take place in a certain year, but the bulk of the expenses took place the year before. This is why a benchmark, such as other companies with legal teams that are the same size and in the same industry, can be used for comparative purposes in order the reduce large variances and make yearly ROI more uniform. Benchmarks provide a more accurate picture of ROI, and they help leaders feel that their legal teams are valuable.

Circumstantial savings - It is difficult to measure the value of successful risk management. For example, attorneys might negotiate the terms of a contract that reduces liability for their organization. If liability was avoided, then it never existed...so how can it be measured? In reality, it cannot be measured...and that is why circumstances need to be taken into account when calculating the costs involved. Astute leaders understand circumstantial savings, and they use them to help determine the value of their legal teams.

The third measure of determining value is the achievement of organizational goals. Legal teams need to contribute toward the accomplishment of goals or they will not earn their keep. In fact, legal teams should be the driving force for goal accomplishment because they focus on company strategies. Organizational leaders need to realize their legal teams' involvement in strategy and allow their lawyers to make decisions. These decisions, good or bad, can then be used to determine value because they affect the goals of the organization.

The last measure for defining the value of attorneys is purely psychological. It involves the amount of stress employees are experiencing since that stress impacts workplaces dramatically. Employees' reactions to stress are different because some are able to handle it in larger doses than others. However, it must be remembered that employee reactions are their reality...and the stress they feel is real. If workers experience less stress due to the legal team, then the legal team has value. If stress levels remain the same or go up, then the legal team needs to show its value in other ways.

In short, a legal team in an organization is a department by itself. It has objectives, but it is typically not an income generator so it has to show how it adds value. If it shows value, it will grow and prosper...but if value cannot be established, then it will cease to exist.

Now that you understand the meaning of value for legal teams, let's move on. The next section involves managing lawyers so they can perform to the best of their potential. Management might be the most challenging part of having in-house legal teams because organizational leaders have to be careful of what they say or do...as is shown in the following section.

Managing

Attorneys on legal teams possess a wealth of legal knowledge...typically more than anyone else in the organization. That being said, it can be a challenge to manage them because they often think that they know what should be done in any legal situation. So, what is the best way to manage attorneys? Interestingly, the answer can be very simple or quite complex, depending on the path chosen. If leaders try to tell their attorneys what to do, they may become offended and think about leaving the organization. However, if those same leaders try to be exercise hands-off management, then the attorneys might feel like they are not getting the proper support to do their jobs.

Lawyers must meet the needs of their employer while having the freedom to take action the way they see best for the situation. They work best when management establishes a culture of mutual respect and collaboration. To achieve this culture, organizational leaders must adhere to the following basic principles:

> *Appreciation* - Some members of legal teams appear to be arrogant and narcissistic. This might actually be true in some cases, but many times they are perceived as such because their work is completely different from most of their coworkers and that work is often confidential. They cannot divulge their knowledge of certain situations, and this makes them seem as if they are privileged and better than everyone else. However, anyone else in the same position would behave the same way or risk losing their job.
>
> In reality, attorneys are employees who experience many of the same problems as their coworkers. They have good and bad days, and they sometimes need a little help getting motivated. Astute leaders realize this need and express gratitude to show that they care about the attorneys and their problems. In short, a pat on the back goes a long way in terms of appreciation...and that is why it is an important aspect of managing legal teams.
>
> *Workloads* - Attorneys often work long days because they know they will be handsomely compensated for their efforts. However, many of these individuals move into the corporate world so they can escape the long hours and establish more of a work-life balance. Unfortunately, some find that they are still required to work long hours in order to get the job done. Leaders need to realize their lawyers need personal time and their jobs must allow for that time. Workloads need to be limited in order to find work-life balance and that is why they are important for proper management of attorneys.
>
> *Spending* – Regardless of the value of legal teams, they need to have spending limits. For this reason, they are best managed by having some type of budget in place. This budget can be re-evaluated and changed after time, but it must exist because companies have many other expenses aside from those associated with legal activities. Leaders typically understand the need to control spending, but it can get out of line in a very short period of time if it is not monitored.
>
> *Creativity* – Some problems are not solved with tradition solutions. For example, bathroom rights of transgender people are hazy in terms of legality because there are differing opinions on the subject. Traditional thinking separates men and women, but this is not an acceptable

resolution in many people's minds. Creative thinkers have suggested a third bathroom that is not gender specific as a solution to the problem. This might or might not work, but it is an example of thinking "outside of the box."

Attorneys on legal teams need the freedom to think "outside the box" in order to come up with resolutions for certain legal issues. They need to be creative or problems do not get solved and costs increase. For this reason, leaders of organizations need to give legal departments some freedom to be creative or be prepared to suffer the potential consequences.

Knowledge – Attorneys typically are hired by companies because they possess knowledge that is lacking in the workforce. This knowledge must be respected because it is critical for resolution of legal issues. Leaders who fail to recognize the power of knowledge will end up where they started before they hired legal teams…but with less money and more frustration.

Style – There are many different types of management styles including authoritarian, democratic, laissez-fair, paternalistic, transactional, and transformation. Each of these styles differs in terms of the methodology used to get people to do what needs to be done. However, regardless of the style used to manage legal teams, it needs to be geared toward project management because attorneys typically see their work as projects. Leaders must understand this need because the efficiency of the team is dependent upon it.

Risk – Risk mitigating is the major reason companies have legal teams. However, the presence of a legal team does not guarantee that problems will be resolved as hoped for or planned. There are situations, such as the loss of a lawsuit, where negative risk turns into reality and the organization suffers. Leaders need to understand that they will come out on the short end of some situations and this setback cannot be completely blamed on the legal team. In terms of risk, it needs to be shared between the legal team and organizational leaders or that legal team is not being properly managed.

Now you understand how to manage legal teams in order to make them perform at peak levels. However, there are also other ways to make these teams better…and that is why improvement is the focus of the next section.

Improving

Like every other aspect of organizations, legal teams can be improved. This is accomplished with understanding and implementation of the following:

Limit diversification – This refers to legal teams being "all things to everybody." They simply cannot do this because their knowledge base is not that extensive. This is not belittling the attorneys on the teams, it is merely saying that they do not and cannot know everything. Based on this fact, legal teams can be improved if leaders limit the diversity of the projects under their jurisdiction.

Set clear goals – Virtually everyone who has worked in an organization understands that their jobs are made harder if management has not established clear goals. Without goals, employees are not sure what direction they need to take or what needs to be accomplished. Believe it or not, this also applies to the attorneys on in-house legal teams. People tend to think of attorneys as leaders who make decisions and establish direction. In many instances, this is true…but it is not the reality for every situation. If leaders want their legal departments to improve, then they need to clearly define the goals and objectives they have for the attorneys involved.

Educate clients – This improvement suggestion is not a mistake! Educating clients is a necessary part of improving in-house legal teams. Attorneys usually require help to resolve issues, and clients can provide that help if they understand what they need to do. For example, if asked to do so, a client can provide critical testimony on an embezzlement issue that they personally witnessed. This is valuable information for prosecuting attorneys, and they could never have obtained it without the client's assistance. If attorneys invest a little time and effort into educating their clients, the legal teams they are part of will improve in quality while reducing the time they need to resolve issues.

Establish think tanks – Think tanks are essentially groups of people that get together to discuss issues and bounce ideas off each other. These groups can be formal, such as committees or forums, or informal, such as employee meetings, but they must be held in order to extract the thoughts of everyone who has knowledge of the subject matter. Think tanks identify problems and help prevent them from festering into larger issues. They also point out things that the legal team might not know. For example, attorneys might not understand how a specific manufacturing process works, and that information is necessary for a project they are working on. In short, think tanks work well for improving in-house legal teams, and smart leaders use them on a regular basis.

Outsource legal expertise – At first glance, this might seem rather ridiculous. After all, in-house legal teams are assembled to reduce the external legal costs that were accruing before the teams existed. However, there are areas outside of the team's expertise regardless of the number of attorneys on staff. For example, a specialized attorney might be needed for food labeling regulations in a different country. If the case warrants outside legal counsel, then that council needs to be hired. Leaders who understand this need will improve their in-house legal departments while helping them learn new things from specialized experts.

Summary

Legal teams in organizations have been growing in popularity with good reason. They provide a service by minimizing the risks of doing business and helping organizations grow and prosper. They are always on the minds of progressive leaders, many of whom have removed them from the wish and made them a reality.

This book discusses legal teams in organizations. It describes how these teams are assembled, examines their objectives, discusses their value, shows how to manage them, and suggests methods for their improvement. The text is informative and educational, and it is written for easy reader understanding at all levels.

Congratulations! You now understand more about in-house legal teams...a welcome addition to many organizations.

Labor Unions in Organizations
Types, Structures, Advantages, and Disadvantages

Louis Bevoc

Published by
NutriNiche System LLC

Louis Bevoc books...simple explanations of complex subjects

Introduction 17
- Wages 17
- Benefits 17
- Job security 19
- Working conditions 20

Types 21
- Industrial 21
- Craft 22
- Public sector 22

Structure 23
- General membership 24
  - Benefits 24
  - Power 24
  - Responsibilities 24
- Executive board 24
- Executive officers 25
  - President 25
  - Vice-president 25
  - Secretary 25
  - Treasurer 26
  - Auditor 26
  - Chief steward 26
  - Steward 27
  - Committees 27

Advantages 28
- Better wages and benefits 28
- Right to grievances 28
- Strength in numbers 28
- Secured jobs 29

Disadvantages 29
- Devaluation of high performers 29
- Abuse 29
- Problems with seniority 29
- Loss of jobs 29

Summary
Introduction

First, a point needs to be clarified about this book. It does not support or oppose unions in workplaces, nor does it argue any position on the topic. It is written for readers to gain a better understanding of union types and structures, and it introduces them to union advantages and disadvantages from an employee standpoint.

Labor unions have lost some power in recent years, but they are still fairly common in businesses across the United States. Certain areas of the country, such as the Northeast and Midwest, have larger percentages of unionized companies, but unions can be found in every state.

Unions represent workers in a variety of different industries in matters involving wage and benefit negotiations, working conditions, and disagreements with management over contract stipulations. However, the most prominent unions today are rooted in the public sector. This is partially due to the fact that unions in private industry have been attacked by special interest groups for having attained too much power of over the past half-century.

Unions are established in organizations after being voted in by employees. A majority of worker votes is needed to solidify the existence of a union, and that union then has the sole authority to negotiate all conditions of employment for its members.

The process used for negotiation is called collective bargaining. Collective bargaining differs from other business negotiations because it is mandated and governed by a variety of external laws and provisions. Collective bargaining also differs from other types of negotiations because the parties involved must continue working together after finalizing the contract. Management and union representatives need to resolve disagreements based on the stipulations of the contract, and this can be difficult if personnel on either side dislike each other.

Typically unions negotiate the following for employees:

Wages

Most workers want to earn more money…and that is why wages are critical for unions to negotiate. A union's goal is to increase employee wages to a level that the union perceives as fair. Once wages are negotiated and finalized, they become part of the union contract. The contract must be followed by management or the company could face legal action to mandate compliance.

Benefits

Unions negotiate all employee benefits, and this can be more involved than many people might think. Benefits negotiated can include any of the following:

- Health insurance

This is insurance for the general health of employees and their families. It generally provides coverage for all health issues except those related to eyes or teeth, and it includes many different types of specialists.

- *Dental insurance*

    This is insurance for the teeth related health of employees and their families. It includes generalists and different types of specialists.

- *Vision insurance*

    This is insurance for the eye-related health of employees and their families.

- *Life insurance*

    This is insurance for employees if they die. If they pass away, the money from the insurance is given to their designated beneficiaries.

- *Long-term disability insurance*

    This is insurance for employees if they become disabled for long periods of time.

- *Short-term disability insurance*

    This is insurance for employees if they become disabled for short periods of time.

- *Paid sick days*

    This is pay that employees receive when they are sick and cannot come to work.

- *Paid personal days*

    This is pay that employees receive when they need time off for personal reasons. It is in addition to paid vacation and paid sick days.

- *Paid vacation*

    This is pay that employees receive when they take time off for vacations.

- *Paid holidays*

    This is pay given to employees when they do not work on designated holidays.

- *Paid pregnancy leave*

    This is pay given to employees who miss work due to pregnancy.

- *Pension programs*

    These programs provide income for employees after they retire.

- *401K programs (including company match)*

    These are tax deferred retirement programs that employees can contribute to during each pay period. The money they contribute is sometimes matched by their employer.

- *Profit sharing programs*

    These programs provide money in addition to regular pay, but they are based on the profitability of the organization.

- *Gain sharing programs*

    These programs provide money in addition to regular pay, but they are not based on the profitability of the organization. Instead, employees need to meet designated goals in order to receive payouts.

- *Bonus programs*

    These programs give money to employees at the end of a specific amount of time based on performance.

- *Stock ownership programs*

    These programs allow employees to purchase stock below the market value.

- *Work-life balance programs*

    These programs are designed to help employees find a balance between work and personal life. An example is telecommuting.

- *Employee discount programs*

    These programs are discounts given to employees for designated products or services.

From the above list, it's rather obvious that the term "benefits" has many different applications.

Job Security

Workers want job security with their employer, and that is one of the reasons they vote unions into their organizations. Unions prevent "at will" employment (situations where employees can be terminated without establishing "just cause") and make it harder for employers to terminate employees for reasons that are illegitimate or superficial. Some of these reasons include:

- *The employee is not fast enough*
- *The employee is not working hard enough*
- *The employee did not listen to instructions*
- *The employee is not friendly*
- *The employee does not fit in*
- *The employee is not well-liked*

Employees guilty of the above infractions might ultimately be terminated in the long run, but union contracts have formal procedures in place that need to be adhered to before the termination can take place. These procedures include warnings and suspensions that follow a specific progression.

Working Conditions

Unions fight to improve workplace safety and overall working conditions. Some of their actions include:

- *Regulating workplace temperatures*

    Unions try to assure workplaces are heated or air-conditioned if working temperatures are a concern. For example, job shops in Minnesota should be heated in the winter, and assembly plants in Florida should be air-conditioned in the summer.

    However, there are limitations to union intervention regarding workplace temperatures. Extreme hot and cold environments cannot always be controlled due to mandatory requirements or the nature of the situation. For example, smelting plants are going to be hot due to the environment, and meat freezers need to be cold for food safety reasons. In these situations, unions are not able to fight for changes…so instead they work toward getting employees more frequent breaks.

- *Regulating workplace lighting*

    Employees need to be able to see what they are doing in order to perform their jobs properly and prevent accidents from occurring. Unions do research to discover recommended lighting levels, and then they work towards forcing companies to comply with those recommendations.

- *Requiring safety equipment*

    Some jobs require safety gear such as special shoes, helmets, or gloves. Unions designate gear that is needed to keep employees safe and then work towards forcing companies to supply that gear.

- *Requiring cleaner work areas*

    Clean work areas are often needed for productivity and safety reasons. Unions push organizations to maintain work areas in a clean or sanitary manner so the conditions are better for their members.

- *Requiring periodic breaks*

    Unions want to make sure employees are well rested in order to properly perform the functions of their jobs. They work toward getting companies to supply frequent or longer breaks for their members.

Now that you have a basic understanding of what labor unions attempt to do for employees, let's move into the specific types of unions that exist in the United States.

Types

Unions reached their peak in the mid-20th century. Membership has declined since that point, but unions still influence the way many organizations operate and conduct business.

Essentially, there are three types of unions in the United States. These unions are:

Industrial

Description

Industrial unions generally represent workers in specific industries, regardless of the jobs they perform. They have more members than craft unions because craft unions are limited to individual trades or skills.

Types of industries that elect industrial unions include:

- Transportation
- Distribution
- Warehousing
- Construction
- Food
- Chemical
- Power

Industrial unions are considered better unions than craft unions due to the following:

- Industrial unions have greater bargaining power during contract negotiations because they have more members than craft unions.
- Industrial unions have more leverage during strikes because they have more members than craft unions.

- Industrial unions remain united at all times. This is not the case for craft unions because they are most concerned about the well-being of their own members.
- Industrial unions are not divided. Craft unions tend to fight over jurisdiction and the right to strike.
- Industrial unions members do not cross picket lines. Craft union members often have the freedom to cross each other's picket lines. In fact, some craft union contracts require members to cross picket lines of other unions.

Craft

Description

Craft unions typically represent workers in a specific trade or occupation. This includes workers in skilled trades.

Occupations that elect craft unions include:

- Electricians
- Millwrights
- Plumbers
- Welders
- Pipe fitters
- Machinists

Craft unions are considered better unions than industrial unions due to the following:

- Craft unions are able to get higher wages for specifically skilled workers. Industrial unions have to negotiate the group as a whole, so skilled workers lose to compensate unskilled workers.
- Craft unions fight harder for every worker because memberships are smaller. Industrial unions have large memberships and workers might not get left out.
- Craft unions control apprenticeships, and they can create a shortage of skilled workers in order to drive up wages. Industrial unions do not have apprenticeships to control, and they cannot drive up wages by creating shortages of workers.
- Craft unions control apprenticeships, and they can select the best individuals to assure the union continues. Industrial unions do not have apprentices to control, and they cannot select the best individuals to assure the union continues.
- Craft unions control the content of jobs and the skills needed to perform those jobs. Industrial unions cannot control the content or skills of their member's jobs.

Public Sector

Description

This is the largest type of union in the United States. It represents government workers, regardless of their job.

Workers in public sector unions include:

- Police officers
- Firefighters
- Postal workers
- Sanitation workers
- Teachers

Public sector unions are considered better unions than industrial unions or craft unions due to the following:

- Contract negotiations are based on government budgets...and governments rarely ever go bankrupt or shut down. Craft union and industrial union negotiations are based on the financial stability of private corporations...and private corporations go bankrupt and shut down on a regular basis.
- Public sector unions have national exposure and often get public support or sympathy nationwide. Craft unions and industrial unions rarely get public support or sympathy on a national level.
- Public sector unions are growing in membership as craft unions and industrial unions decline in membership. This gives public sector unions more negotiating power than craft unions or industrial unions.

Now that you have an understanding of the three basic types of unions, let's move into the structure of unions in general.

Structure

Unions have similar structures, but those structures are tailored toward the goals and objectives of the specific union. For example, a craft union for teachers would have a mission that is different from that of an industrial union in a food processing plant. The teachers' union might have a goal of reducing class sizes, while the food processing union wants to add more employees to the workforce.

Along the same lines, a police officers' public sector union would have a different mission than an electricians' craft union. The police officers' union might have a goal of increasing protective equipment for officers on the streets, while the electricians' union has an objective of eliminating holiday work.

Unions of the same type can also have differing objectives. Consider two types of occupations in the public sector unions - firefighters and sanitation workers. The firefighters' union might want members to work a maximum of one weekend per month, while the sanitation workers' union wants to reduce the maximum weight of refuse they are required to lift from 40 pounds to 35 pounds.

In short, goals and philosophies of different unions reflect the needs of their members. However, the structure of all unions can be broken down into four major areas. These areas include the general membership, executive board, executive officers, and committees. Each area is described below and broken down into smaller components for a more detailed understanding.

General membership

General members are the reason unions are formed. They are the beneficiaries of union activity, and their needs rank above all other concerns. They are also the most powerful decision making force within the union, and they control its destiny. However, this power comes with responsibilities that involve understanding union objectives and getting involved with union actions.

Below is a closer examination of the role of general membership within the union:

Benefits

- They are entitled to union education and training.
- They are entitled to union grievance support.
- They are entitled to union legal assistance when necessary.

Power

- They elect people to important union positions including the executive board and executive officers.
- They approve policies and procedures regarding union management.
- They approve changes in union leadership.

Responsibilities

- They need to understand the by-laws and constitution of the union.
- They need to participate in internal and external union activities.
- They need to pay dues for their union membership.

Executive board

This is the next level up from general membership on the union's hierarchical ladder. Members at this level make sure that approved policies and procedures are implemented and carried out in the manner designated by the general members.

The executive board plays an important role in the union because it ensures the general member's wishes are adhered to properly. Without this board, the guidelines voted in by general members would be essentially useless, and anarchy could be the end result.

Additionally, the executive board considers the general members to be shareholders in the union. Like a board of directors in a business, they report on all union activities so general members are kept abreast of internal and external happenings.

Executive officers

This group consists of the president, vice-president, secretary, treasurer, auditors, chief steward, and stewards. Once elected by the general members, they are responsible for the daily functioning of the union. This entails being involved in virtually every aspect of daily operations to assure the union works for members in order to attain higher wages, better benefits, and improved working conditions.

Each officer has specific responsibilities in regard to union operations, and those responsibilities are as follows:

President

The president is the main person responsible for the daily operations of the union. If the union is not achieving designated goals or objectives, then the president is responsible. In short, the president is accountable for the union's maintenance, growth, and prosperity.

Other responsibilities of the president often include:

- Acts as chief external union communicator
- Acts as chief internal union communicator
- Acts as chief union negotiator
- Acts as chief union arbitrator
- Oversees union executive board meetings
- Oversees union finances (P&L, budgets, expenses, etc.)
- Directs union executive officers
- Directs union general membership
- Signs all important union documents

Vice-president

Similar to the vice-president of the United States, the vice-president assumes the president's responsibilities if he or she is unable to do so. He or she also handles other tasks assigned by the president.

Other responsibilities of the vice-president often include:

- Acts as chair of the grievance committee
- Acts as advisor to chief steward and stewards
- Coordinates union benefits
- Coordinates union training

Secretary

The secretary is responsible for all clerical duties. This involves maintaining and storing all records, files, and data related to union activities.

Other responsibilities of the secretary often include:

- Writes or records minutes at union meetings. Minutes are official records of union actions that are permanently filed.
- Writes official union letters.
- Opens union mail (letter, bills, etc.) and delivers to appropriate officers

Treasurer

The treasurer handles many financial aspects of the union's daily operations. He or she monitors union funds for accuracy and discrepancies and maintains all financial transaction records. In short, the treasurer is a safeguard for union funds.

Other responsibilities of the treasurer often include:

- Prepares budget
- Manages assets
- Assures dues are collected
- Arranges for audits

Auditor

The auditor conducts audits of union financial activities over specific periods of time. This assures that monetary transactions are consistent with the goals and objectives of the union. In short, the auditor is a safeguard for making sure union finances reflect the goals of the organization.

Specific aspects of union financial activities examined during an audit often include:

- Wages
- Expense reports
- Credit card charges
- Allowances
- Receipts
- Disbursements
- Government reports
- Union reports
- Record maintenance

Chief steward

A chief steward assists lower level stewards in their daily activities. These individuals are typically seasoned union officials, and they serve the role of a mentor.

Other responsibilities of the chief steward often include:

- Educates new stewards on handling grievances
- Identifies member concerns and creates plans of action for addressing
- Oversees steward committee meetings

Steward

The steward is on the front line for member grievances. These individuals receive the grievances and process them using the standard union protocol.

Other responsibilities of the steward often include:

- Educates members on union policies and procedures
- Organizes union meetings with members
- Serves as union contact for disputes with company management

Committees

Unions have a variety of committees that utilize members from all levels of the hierarchy. These committees have different functions, but essentially they are designed to provide members with guidance, direction, and understanding in regards to union policies and procedures.

The following are examples of committees that are often formed by unions:

Organizing committee

This committee coordinates the efforts of the organizing process. It involves employees at all levels of the union, and it requires member commitment.

Education and training committee

This committee educates members on union programs, policies, and procedures. In short, it educates employees on their rights and responsibilities as union members.

Budget/finance committee

This committee serves as a watchdog over union money to assure it is used appropriately.

Legal Committee

This committee is in charge of any legal actions that take place within the union.

Information committee

This committee provides the union with information needed for negotiations. Members do research to gather facts and data that can be used to support the union's position.

Negotiation committee

This committee represents the union in negotiations with management. They establish goals based on the feedback they receive from members.

Grievance committee

This committee works to resolve disputes and conflicts between members and management.

Community services committee

This committee gets the union involved in the community to support causes they deem worthwhile.

Retirees committee

This committee has a dual purpose. First, it organizes retirees to gain their support for the union. Then it gives back to the retirees by supporting community service programs that they value.

Now you have a basic understanding of union types and their structure. Let's expand upon that knowledge in the next section by discussing the pros and cons of unions from an employee perspective.

Advantages

Unions are advantageous to employees for the following reasons:

Better wages and benefits

Unions fight for improved wages and benefits for their members. This often results in better compensation packages than workers who perform similar jobs in non-union plants.

Right to grievances

Union employees have the right to argue their position if they feel they have been wronged by the company. They simply file a grievance with the union steward, and the union fights on their behalf. Employees in non-union companies do not always have the option to argue their position because management's decision is final.

Strength in numbers

Unions have an advantage based on the number of members they have fighting for a common cause. In short, it's easier for a group of people to get a company to change than it is for any single person.

Secured jobs

Management in union companies cannot fire workers for any reason. A strict protocol must be followed in order to terminate an employee, and this provides job security for union members.

Disadvantages

Unions are disadvantageous to employees for the following reasons:

Devaluation of high performers

Many people believe that higher performing employees deserve higher pay. This is not possible in a union environment because workers at the same level are compensated equally.

Abuse

Unions were necessary when workers started to organize many years ago. Workplace conditions were often terrible, and management had no restrictions on how employees were treated. However, those type of workplace conditions are few and far between in the modern world because laws are in place to prevent them from existing. Today's unions often end up fighting for those members who abuse their protection. Some union employees are aware that companies have great difficulty firing them, and because of this, they abuse the system so it works to their advantage.

Problems with seniority

Unions reward employees based on seniority. Skills and qualifications are not taken into account when positions become available, and this means the best people are not always chosen for the job.

Loss of jobs

Unions do a good job increasing wages and benefits for their members. However, these increases can put financial burdens on companies that cannot be overcome. When companies shut down because they are no longer profitable, everyone loses...including union members.

Summary

Labor unions have been a hot topic of discussion in the United States for many years because once voted in, they have sole authority to negotiate all conditions of employment for their members. They represent members in matters involving wages, benefits, working conditions, and disagreements with management over contract stipulations. Although unions have lost some power in recent years, they are still fairly common in organizations across the United States.

This book helps readers gain a better understanding of union types, structures, advantages, and disadvantages. It does not support or oppose unions in workplaces, nor does it arguing any position on the topic. The goal is simply to educate readers about unions so they can formulate their own opinions.

Congratulations! You now understand more about labor unions...an important aspect of organizational behavior.

Negotiation in Organizations
Skills, Tactics, Mistakes, and Improving

Louis Bevoc

Published by
NutriNiche System LLC

Louis Bevoc books...simple explanations of complex subjects

Introduction — 34
- What is negotiation? — 34
- Why is negotiation important? — 34
- Why is a win-win negotiation outcome desirable? — 34

Skills — 35
- Planning — 35
- Assuming — 36
- Asking — 36
- Understanding — 36
- Listening — 36
- Observing — 37
- Communicating — 37
- Controlling — 37
- Deciding — 37
- Resolving — 37

Tactics — 38
- Offering — 38
- Combining — 39
- Bartering — 39
- Waiting — 39
- Sectioning — 39
- Prioritizing — 40
- Questioning — 40
- Agreeing — 41
- Walking — 41

Mistakes
- 41
- Failing to plan — 42
- Failing to listen or observe — 42
- Failing to keep an open mind — 43
- Failing to recognize one's own behavior — 43
- Failing to hold composure — 43

Improving — 44
- Listen and observe — 44
- Adjust — 44

Plan and prepare 45
Summary 45

Introduction

A discussion about negotiation is best started by asking some critical questions:

What is negotiation?

It is a process where people settle their differences by coming to an agreement. The goal is to reach that agreement with compromise from both sides. There will be some disagreement, but arguing should be minimal with the focus being on principle rather than position.

Why is negotiation important?

It is important because conflicts arise due to different viewpoints, wants, and needs. Without it, people would argue to no end, dislike each other, and be dissatisfied. Negotiation allows people to reach agreements that satisfy everyone involved.

This does not mean that people will get exactly what they want. It means that will get some things they want while compromising on others. If done correctly, negotiation creates a win-win situation.

Why is a win-win negotiation outcome desirable?

Some people believe that they are right, their opposition is wrong, and there is no compromise. For these people, a win-lose situation is the only option. In other words, they win and their opposition loses.

The win-lose mentality is not good because it clearly establishes winners and losers. It does not allow losers to "save face," and this can create a major communication barrier down the line. Losers might be too mad or embarrassed to face winners, and this prevents the two parties from working together in the future.

Win-win situations are almost always better than win-lose situations, but it must also be remembered that the goal of each party is to negotiate an outcome that is best for their interests. This thinking can be applied to negotiation in organizations. For example, a union wants what is best for their members while management wants what is best for the company.

Negotiation occurs in organizations for a variety of reasons. When conflicts arise, they need to be resolved...and negotiation is the best process to achieve that resolution. Without some type of negotiation process, warring factions never cease. This negatively impacts workplaces in terms of growth and prosperity, and it can lead to an organization's demise.

This book is about understanding and improving negotiation in organizations. It examines negotiation skills, strategies, and mistakes with the goal of showing readers how to improve their techniques and create win-win situations where both sides feel they gained something.

Now that you have a basic understanding of negotiation, let's move on to the next section that discusses essential negotiation skills.

Skills

An important fact about negotiation skills is the following:

People who are not born with negotiation skills can learn them and become effective negotiators.

This fact needs to be understood because some people believe they are not capable of negotiating. This is simply not true because anyone who is capable of learning is capable of learning negotiating skills. They might not be the best negotiators, but they can do it as long as they are willing to put forth the necessary time and effort. Please consider the following as support:

People who are naturally persuasive might be better negotiators than those who are not naturally persuasive. However, preparation can partially substitute for persuasion because it gives people knowledge. Knowledge establishes credibility, and credible people are persuasive.

Negotiation skills evolve from many different factors. All of these factors cannot be discussed in the scope of this book, but some of the major ones are listed below.

Planning

This might be the most important factor because planning prepares people for the entire negotiating process. Well planned negotiations have a much better chance of being successful than poorly planned negotiations.

Planning involves:

Determining goals and objectives

Know your objectives and the other party's objectives. Think about ideal outcomes, acceptable outcomes, and unacceptable outcomes to the negotiation.

Conducting research

Learn as much as possible about the other party. Try to figure out what techniques and ideas can be used to influence their thinking. Also, try to find similar negotiations and examine the outcomes for possible relationships.

Defining information limitations

Determine the information that can be revealed to the other party and the information that needs to be kept confidential. This is important because some information can be used by the other party to strengthen their leverage in the negotiation process.

Preparing an agenda

Decide the order in which issues need to be discussed. Sometimes the least significant concerns are discussed first in order to lead up to the more important ones, and other times the opposite occurs so the most important issues are discussed first. The order depends on the agenda...and that is why the agenda needs to be planned.

The best way to think about planning is to remember the old saying, "Those who fail to plan, plan to fail."

Assuming

Never assume something is fact. In other words, avoid any type of bias during the negotiation. Try to find out exactly what the other party is looking for in the outcome. For example, school administrators might assume that a teacher's union is trying to negotiate higher wages for their members when the union's actual goal is to prevent a loss of benefits.

Asking

Avoid aggressive statements, ask open-ended questions, and focus on the other party's interests. Examples of these are as follows:

Aggressive vs. non-aggressive

Incorrect: This does not benefit us.
Correct: How is this beneficial to us?

Closed-ended vs. open-ended

Incorrect: Are wages your major concern?
Correct: What is your major concern?

Focus on one's own party vs. focus on the other party

Incorrect: The proposed health insurance plan is good for us because we save money.
Correct: The proposed health insurance plan is good for you because you have more options.

Understanding

Identify the reason for the negotiation, isolate the problems involved, and pinpoint areas for compromise. People who fail to understand these aspects of negotiation waste time and frustrate the other party.

Listening

Unfortunately, many people would rather hear themselves speak than listen to others. During negotiations, those who are speaking cannot listen to what is being said by the other party....and they miss hearing important information that could be used to reach a compromise.

In short, listening is a learned skill that is often more important than speaking during negotiation. Maybe this is why people are born with two ears and only one mouth!

Observing

Similar to listening, observation is an important skill for negotiating. Watch the other party's gestures and reactions to determine if they are nervous, excited, or upset. Non-verbal communication provides a wealth of information that can be used to reach a compromise.

In short, actions often speak louder than words. It's simply a matter of interpreting those actions.

Communicating

This is necessary for preventing misunderstanding. Negotiators must convey their desired goals and the reasons why those goals are justifiable, and this is done through effective communication with the other party. Without effective communication, negotiations become confusing and frustrating...and compromises sometimes fail to be reached.

Controlling

Controlling refers to emotions. People need to control their emotions during negotiations or they risk failing to achieve their objectives. Unfortunately, this is not always easy to do because negotiations can bring out frustration, irritation, anger, happiness, relief, joy, and many other feelings related to emotions...especially if the discussion gets personal.

It is always best to keep emotions in check during negotiations. While this can be difficult, it is possible. Sometimes all it takes is the practice that comes with experience.

Deciding

People need to be able to make decisions during negotiations. Wishy-washy negotiators waste valuable time and often upset the other party in the process. This skill is especially important for compromising because opportunities arise instantaneously...and they disappear just as quickly.

One good thing about decision making is the fact that it gets better with experience. Being involved in this aspect of a negotiation pays dividends the next time around.

Resolving

This involves being able to resolve problems as the negotiation moves forward. People who focus only on their goals lose sight of other aspects of the negotiation...and that includes problems that develop along the way. For example, a buyer has a specific goal of spending no more than $10,000 for a machine. During negotiations with the machine manufacturer, the buyer makes this very clear. The manufacturer tells him they make a machine for this price, but it will not be available for nine months. The buyer needs the machine in three months, but he ignores that need and buys it because the price is right.

The buyer based his decision on his goals rather than trying to resolve the logistics problem. The deal he negotiated will bring the machine in too late for the needs of his organization. In short, he used poor negotiating skills.

Now that you understand some important factors related to negotiation skills, let's move on to negotiation tactics in the next section.

Tactics

Negotiation needs a plan of action, and tactics are an important part of that plan. Tactics use the skills discussed in the previous section to achieve designated goals and objectives.

The following are some effective tactics used during negotiation:

Offering

This tactic involves making the first offer. It's very difficult to determine which party should make the first offer in a negotiation. However, one rule to follow is to never make the first offer without knowing the real value of the subject being negotiated. For example, consider two scenarios for a woman business owner who is negotiating with the union that represents her employees:

Scenario #1

She knows that the average wage in her industry is $15 per hour, so she makes the first offer of $13.50 per hour. This makes sense because she knows where she wants the wages to end up. She has knowledge of the situation and her tactic of making the first offer is justified.

Scenario #2

She does not know anything about long-term care insurance for her employees because the concept is relatively new. Since she is unsure what to do, she decides to offer a $150 per month toward long-term care packages for every employee. This makes no sense because she has no knowledge of the situation, and her tactic of making the first offer is not justified.

Combining

This tactic involves offering multiple incentives to reach an agreement. For example:

> A builder is working with a customer to add an addition to her retail store. The customer wants the addition, but she hesitates due to the cost. As an added incentive, the builder offers to purchase and install all of the shelving for her store at no extra charge. She accepts the offer and the plan moves forward.

In this case, the tactic of combining was successful because both parties believed they accomplished their goals.

Bartering

This tactic involves trading one incentive for another in order to reach an agreement. For example:

> Management at a manufacturing plant is negotiating a new contract with the union. The plant only needs 11 millwrights based on production volume, but the union wants to maintain the jobs of the current 15 millwrights. Management agrees to keep the 15 jobs open in exchange for the union allowing the millwright's wages to be frozen for the next three years.

In this case, the tactic of bartering was successful because each party believed they accomplished their goals.

Waiting

This tactic involves patience. Specifically, it refers to waiting before responding to an offer. It uses time to show (1) there is no urgency and (2) other options are available. It also keeps the other side wondering if they offered enough incentive to reach an agreement.

Sectioning

Some negotiations fall apart because one or both of the parties refuse to compromise. They take an "all or nothing" approach and fail to reach an agreement. When this happens, both parties walk away unhappy.

A tactic used to deal with an "all or nothing" situation involves breaking the negotiations into smaller sections and dealing with each section on an individual basis. For example:

> Management at a food processing company is in contract negotiations with the union representing truck drivers. One of the issues is that the union does not want drivers to work on Sundays because they need time to be with their families. However, management must have drivers work on Sunday because products need to reach the stores on a daily basis.

Both parties are unwilling to budge on this issue, so they decide to separately work on another area of the contract. They discuss the wage and benefit packages for the drivers and reach an agreement that out of pocket insurance costs will not rise for the next two years and wages will be limited to a three percent increase. This agreement does not resolve the Sunday work issue, but it completes the wage and benefit part of the contract negotiation.

In this case, the tactic of sectioning allowed the parties to reach an agreement on a certain aspect of the negotiation, and it helped everyone feel like some progress was being made toward a resolution.

Prioritizing

This tactic establishes important aspects of the negotiation process including:

Separating business from personal

This expands upon the controlling factor discussed in the skills section. Negotiators need to focus on facts rather than their emotions. Emotional reactions can be very strong and work against the goals and objectives trying to be achieved. This is why business facts need to be prioritized over personal feelings during negotiations.

Determining issue significance

Issues are sometimes placed in order of importance in order to establish agendas that have the best chance of achieving goals and objectives. This allows negotiators to give more attention to top priorities in the beginning. For example:

> Hourly wages are the most important concern for fast food workers, so they are discussed first and foremost during contract negotiations. Issues related to health care and paid holidays take a back seat until the wages aspect is resolved.

Taking the reins

This involves people taking control of the agenda for the negotiations. Location, size of room, time limits, and number of negotiators all fall into this category. Some of these factors might not seem significant, but they can play an important role. It's comparable to a home field advantage for a sports team.

Questioning

This expands upon the asking factor discussed in the skills section. Negotiators should ask questions rather than make concrete statements that result in arguments. For example:

> Incorrect: Your offer is completely useless to us.
> Correct: Can you tell me how your offer benefits to us?

Incorrect: This will work well for you.
Correct: Will this work well for you?

Incorrect: You obviously do not understand our offer.
Correct: Would you like me to clarify our offer?

Always remember that questions open people up for discussion, and concrete statements shut them down.

Agreeing

This tactic is one of the most basic, but it is often ignored by people who are negotiating. It involves keeping an open mind in order to achieve acceptable solutions to problems. For example:

> A small business owner is negotiating the purchase of a new copy machine with the vice president of sales at the copier company. He cannot afford to buy the machine, so he suggests an alternative method of payment. He offers to buy all copier paper and supplies from the copier company at double the price until the machine is paid off. The vice president of sales has never done this before, but she decides to accept the offer.

In this case, the small business owner thought of an alternative way to pay for the copy machine. The vice president of sales kept an open mind regarding his offer, and she decided to accept it.

In terms of the agreeing tactic, remember the old adage, "a mind is like a parachute, it does not work unless it is open."

Walking

This tactic is used when the negotiation process fails and an agreement cannot be reached. Typically a future meeting is scheduled for further negotiation. This allows both sides to rethink their position and come back to the table with a new or different perspective.

The walking tactic should be a last resort. However, it works well to prevent:

- Heated arguments that result when negotiators disagree
- Wasted time that results when negotiators disagree
- Damaged working relationships that result when negotiators disagree

You are now aware of some major tactics involved in negotiating. These tactics are beneficial for reaching agreements, but people still make common mistakes that damage negotiations. The next section examines those mistakes in detail.

Mistakes

Unfortunately, people make negotiation errors that hinder the development of agreements and compromises.

Common mistakes include the following:

Failing to plan

Plans need to be in place to properly reach an agreement. These plans should account for everything that might happen. While this might appear to be a daunting task, it is doable.

Many negotiators forget about or ignore the following factors that need to be a part of planning:

Research

Research compares similar cases for contrast and comparison purposes. Smart planners think about the following question regarding research:

> What were some similar negotiations, what were the outcomes, and how do they relate to this negotiation?

Agenda

Agenda determines the basic strategy of the meeting. Smart planners think about the following question regarding agenda:

> What issues are top priorities for each side, how much emphasis should be put on each of these, and when should they be discussed?

Goals

Goals are the desired objectives of each side. Smart planners think about the following question regarding goals:

> What are the goals for each side, what are acceptable outcomes, and what unacceptable outcomes?

Options

Options are solutions to a failed negotiation. Smart planners think about the following question regarding alternatives:

> What direction will be taken if an agreement is not reached and how can good working relationships be maintained?

Failing to listen or observe

Please consider the following for each these types of mistakes:

Listening

A noted earlier, some negotiators would rather hear themselves talk than listen to what the other side has to say. This can impact the outcome of negotiations...even to a point where an agreement cannot be reached. A lot more is learned by listening than talking, but some people fail to understand this fact.

Observing

Some negotiators fail to pick up on non-verbal actions from the other side. Slouched body poster, crossed arms, smiles, raised eyebrows, and head shakes are all movements that can indicate people's thoughts. This information can then be used to find common ground and reach compromises.

Failing to keep an open mind

As noted earlier, an open mind is critical for finding alternative ways to reach an agreement. However, some people are unable to think "outside of the box," and this limits their options for problem solving.

Open minded thinking has been a critical aspect of research, innovation, and creativity for centuries. The same philosophy needs to be applied to negotiation...but this is something that many people fail to realize.

Failing to recognize one's own behavior

Many people do not realize the impact of their own behavior during negotiations. They need to understand that their actions are perceived by the other party in different ways...and negative perceptions can prevent an agreement from being reached.

Consider the following examples of behavior in negotiations:

- People who are loud appear to be dominant. The other side views them as rude and aggressive.
- People who are quiet appear aloof. The other side views them as having limited interest.
- People who are nervous appear unprepared or inexperienced. The other side views them as having limited knowledge.
- People who do not make eye contact appear shady. The other side views them as untrustworthy.

In short, negotiators who do not recognize the impact of their own behavior are damaging to themselves and the party they represent.

Failing to hold composure

One last mistake that is often not thought about involves the aftermath of negotiations. Some people celebrate the "victory" after the negotiation is over, and this response risks alienating the other side.

Gloating is unprofessional and it makes the other side seek revenge in future negotiations. In short, negotiators need to think about the impact of their reactions to the final agreement.

Now that you are aware of some of the common mistakes that negotiators make, let's move into the final section on improving negotiation skills.

Improving

Hands down, experience is the best teacher for improving negotiating skills. However, the road to obtaining negotiation experience can be a difficult one to navigate, and people need help along the way. The following three suggestions provide some help to make that road a little easier:

Listen and observe

This book discusses listening and observation as important aspects of negotiation on several occasions. However, there is no overkill here because this point cannot be overemphasized for people engaged in negotiation.

Let's repeat one more time:

- Stop talking
- Listen to what the other side is saying
- Observe the other side's non-verbal behavior

The above three bullets improve people's negotiation skills immediately. Negotiators need to try them to see for themselves how well they work.

Adjust

People need to adjust their communication styles to meet the needs of the other side. This improvement technique expands on listening and observing by going a step further and reacting. People should react to what the other side is saying by responding in the same tone of voice and using similar mannerisms. Mirroring their responses makes them feel more comfortable.

Additionally, emotions need to be kept in check at all times. Nothing hurts agreements more than uncontrolled emotional outbursts.

Think of the other party as a customer who is being sold something. They need to be comfortable with the people on the other side of the negotiating table. If they are not comfortable, they will not buy what is being sold....and there will be no agreement.

Plan and prepare

Planning and preparation are areas that all negotiators can improve upon if they want to invest the time and effort. Think about the following:

- There is more negotiation research that can be conducted for comparison and contrast purposes.
- There are better negotiation agendas that can be formulated.
- There are more options available for negotiations that fail.

People who disagree with the above statements do so because they think they have done enough to plan and prepare. However, they might find out that this is simply not the case after they enter into an important negotiation...and then it is too late.

Summary

Negotiating impacts virtually every organization in the world...and poor negotiation can have disastrous consequences. Based on this, people need to understand how the negotiation process works what can be done to improve it.

This book is about understanding and improving negotiation in organizations. It examines negotiation skills, strategies, and mistakes with the goal of showing readers how to improve their techniques and create win-win situations where both sides feel they gained something. It also uses workplace examples for clarification and better understanding.

Congratulations! You now have a better understanding of workplace negotiation...an important aspect of organizational behavior.

Record Keeping In Organizations
A Basic Understanding

Louis Bevoc

Published by
NutriNiche System LLC

Louis Bevoc books...simple explanations of complex subjects

Introduction 48
- Records management policy 48
- Designating classifications 50
- Assigning responsibilities 51
- Establishing authority 52
- Instituting protocols 53
- Defining life cycles 54
- Electronic vs. paper 55

Reasons 56
- Legality 56
- Ethics 57
- Trends 57
- History 58
- Reference 58

Summary 58

Introduction

In organizations, records provide documented information about actions in the past. They are very important when evidence of what happened is required; thereby preventing "he said, she said" debates and wasted time trying to piece together something from the past. They have been used to convict some people of wrongdoing, and they have also been used to prevent the conviction of others who were falsely accused. Records are needed in a wide variety of situations, and this is a major reason why so many organizations push their employees to keep them accurate and updated...something that will likely never change.

Record keeping might appear to be a rather simple process, but anyone involved with it knows that this perception is not accurate. In fact, record keeping can be quite complex because it requires the management of records from start to finish (creation to destruction). However, before getting into the specifics of records management, organizations need to have a policy in place that addresses records management in general. This policy is discussed below.

Records management policy

A records management policy should include the following sections:

Purpose
Scope
Objectives
Details
Accountably

Each of these sections is defined as follows:

Purpose - This section describes the reasons the policy is being implemented. Why is it needed? How is it beneficial? Most organizations implement these policies for the proper preparation of, storage of, and access to records that might be needed for legal, ethical, historical, trend tracking, or reference purposes.

Scope – This section gives a brief overview of what the policy is going to cover or encompass. What types of records does it cover? Does it cover electronic and paper records? Are multiple facilities covered? The answers to these questions are dependent on the needs of the company, but often times a records management policy covers all records, electronic or paper, generated by the organization at all facilities. This allows the records to be stored and retrieved in a designated area; thereby making security breaches less of a threat and making it easier for authorized people to gain access.

Objectives – What are the goals of the policy? What is hoped to be achieved? This section is typically quite simple and straight-forward, and one or two sentences often do the job. For example, a company's objective might be "to ensure the creation, storage, and security of accurate and authentic records."

Details – This section is the core of the policy. It explains the types of records that will be collected, maintained, and released for review. What records are collected? Where are the records stored? How are the records stored? What records are confidential? Who has access to the records? What is the life cycle of the records? How are the records destroyed? Obviously, there are many different answers to these questions, but they all need to be addressed.

Accountabilities – This section defines responsibilities in regard to the policy. Who will create the records? Who will store the records? Who will make sure the records are secure? Who will determine when the record's life cycles have been completed? Who will destroy the records? The answers to these questions will vary depending on the type or needs of the organization, but they must be addressed for the policy to be successful. Remember, a records management policy is only as good as the people overseeing it…and it cannot oversee itself.

The following is an example of a very basic records management policy for Heidelberg Meat, a small retail store that makes and sells sausage:

Heidelberg Meat's Records Management Policy

Purpose – Heidelberg Meat is maintaining records for the cooking of our products. This is being done because food safety is a top priority and we want to make sure all the sausage we sell our customers is safe for them to consume. We will use these records for governmental, legal, or reference purposes whenever the need arises.

Scope – This policy covers all records generated for sausage cooked in our smokehouses. All of our records are paper, and they will be stored in our building.

Objectives – Our goal is to ensure the creation, storage, and security of accurate records pertaining to the cooking of sausage.

Details – Cooking records containing finished temperatures of our sausage products are collected and stored in a locked file cabinet located in our office. These records are confidential and the only individuals with access are the store owner and the store manager. Records will be destroyed after two years by shredding them.

Accountabilities – The owner or store manager will create the records, store the records in the office file cabinet, make sure the file cabinet is locked, and destroy the records after they have been filed for two years.

Heidelberg Meat's records management policy is short and simple, but the company is small and does not require more complexity. The KISS (Keep It Simple Stupid) strategy should be utilized whenever possible to avoid potential misunderstanding and unnecessary burden on the employees responsible for managing the records.

Now you understand how a records management policy works, and you have seen it exemplified in a small business. Once this type of policy is in place, the specific aspects of records management need to be addressed. These aspects include the following:

Designating classifications

This is a very important aspect that is often overlooked. Some organizations consider every document to be a record, and this is not good. It causes problems right from the start because every record requires time and resources for proper management...and it does not make sense to spend that time and resources on a document that does not need to be a record.

There is a difference between a document and a record. A document is something that, when combined with other documents, makes up a record. It can be an email, tweet, blog, fax, picture, form, file, or another piece of paper. Documents can be changed or updated as needed, so they need to be stored and retrieved, but they are not final. Records are final documents, and they represent some type of action. They require certain protocols to be followed (as discussed below), and they cannot be changed. In short, all records are documents, but not all documents are records. Think of this in terms of the animal kingdom. Seagulls are a type of bird that, along with other types of birds, make up the species. All seagulls are birds, but not all birds are seagulls.

One of the most common ways to classify records is by function. This refers to the function of the record within the organization. Functionally classified records fall into a multi-tiered system that progressively gets more specific. For example, *pay raises* are second tier aspect under the first tier function of *human resources*. Pay raises are then broken down into third tier *hourly raises* and *salary raises*. The complexity of the organization determines the number of tiers for each classification. In general, more complex organizations require more levels of tiers.

Let's look at an example of a functional classification using multi-tiers. Marinelli Cold Press is a coffee manufacturing company with three plants in Detroit (Michigan), Denver (Colorado), and Atlanta (Georgia). Each plant classifies records by departments (functions), with further breakdowns of those functions in subsequent tiers as follows:

> *First-tier* - **The first tier separates** major functions for each manufacturing plant. The Detroit, Denver, and Atlanta plants are each categorized departmentally as shown below.
>
> > Finance
> > Health and Safety
> > Human Resources
> > Inventory Control
> > Sales and Marketing
> > Office
> > Production
> > Quality
> > Shipping and Receiving
> > Training
>
> *Second tier* - **The second tier** subdivides each department into major aspects. For example, the *production* department includes:

Labor
Utilities
Equipment
Raw Materials
In-Process Materials
Finished Product

Third tier - The third tier breaks down each major aspect into specific categories. For example, the equipment aspect includes two specific categories.

Processing
Packaging

Fourth tier- The fourth and final tier divides specific categories into finished products. For example, the packaging type includes two finished products.

Retail
Food Service

Based on the above information, a packaging record for retail coffee manufactured the Chattanooga plant is classified as follows:

Plant	**Chattanooga**	
First-tier	Department	Production
Second tier	Major aspect	Equipment
Third tier	Specific category	Packaging
Fourth tier	Finished product	Retail

If someone needs to locate the packaging records for retail coffee manufactured at the Chattanooga plant, then they know to find it under the function of production.

Functional classification of records is often chosen over other methods, such as alphabetical classification, due to the simplicity it offers. Organizations that file a record alphabetically need to remember the name that was chosen for that record, and this can be challenging when many different records are maintained.

Functional classification also makes retrieval easier when specific categories of records are needed. For example, it is much easier to retrieve sales records filed under the sales department rather than it is to retrieve the sales records filed under each individual product.

Assigning responsibilities

Interestingly, the assignment of responsibilities is involved with record keeping throughout the process. It starts with designating the classification of records and ends with their destruction. In the beginning, someone needs to be assigned the responsibility of deciding which documents are considered to be records. Sometimes, this decision is relatively easy because it is put in writing. For example, government officials designate the records that need to be kept for areas under their jurisdiction. However, every classification decision is not as clear-cut when the government is not involved. One document might support another, so a decision needs to be made as to whether or not one or both documents should be retained. For example, the tempering log for milk chocolate might show that the product reached a temperature of 100 degrees F. This is clearly a record...but is a document showing that the thermometer was properly calibrated also considered a record? The calibration document functions as support that the thermometer is functioning properly; thereby indicating that the final product temperature is accurate, but should it be kept on file? Someone needs to be assigned the responsibility of making that decision.

Protocols also need to be in effect once the records are generated (as discussed below), but someone needs to determine those protocols. Who is responsible for making sure the records are safely stored? Who is required to review the records? Who is authorized to view the records? Who determines when the records are destroyed? These questions need answers, and that is why responsibilities need to be assigned.

Poor decisions on the part of responsible personnel can cause big problems for organizations, sometimes leading to lawsuits or bankruptcy. In certain situations, some employees might even end up going to prison, such as the owner of a chemical company who does not review records that show his company is discharging high levels of pollutants into nearby lakes and streams. Based on these consequences, it is rather obvious that assigning responsibilities is a critical aspect of record keeping.

Establishing authority

Authority and responsibility are not the same when in terms of record keeping. For example, people who are responsible for making sure records are documented do not necessarily have the authority access those records after they are stored. Additionally, people who are authorized to access records are not necessarily responsible for documenting them or storing them. In general, higher confidentially of records equates with fewer people authorized to access and review them.

Many records are required to have restricted access due to privacy, confidentiality, and/or legal reasons. This is discussed in detail in the reasons section of this book, but it is worthy of mention here because it applies to establishing authority. This process often requires safeguards such as passwords for electronic records and access codes for paper records.

One way to restrict access to records is to categorize them by their level of confidentiality and designate authorized people at those levels. An example of a three-level restricted access system is as follows:

Red Level – high confidentiality
Yellow Level – medium confidentiality
Green Level– low confidentiality

In the above system, every employee in the organization is assigned a red, yellow, or green level status, and they are only allowed to access records equal to or below that level. For example, the president and vice president have red level status so they can access all records regardless of confidentiality. Middle managers have yellow level status so they can access medium and low confidentiality records, but they are not allowed access to records consider high confidentiality. Green level status employees are non-supervisory personnel who only have access to low confidentially records.

Interestingly, many government records that have restricted access have that restriction lifted if they are requested via the Freedom of Information Act (FOIA). In 1967, FOIA became a law that provides public access to records from any federal agency upon request unless those records are determined to be exempt for reasons such as national security or personal safety.

FOIA impacts businesses because certain records fall under the jurisdiction of government agencies, so the public has a right to view them. Unfortunately, those records can be damaging to the organizations that are forced to release them because the public's reason for requesting them often involves suspected wrongful activities.

Instituting protocols

Authorized people can view records, but many times they cannot obtain them without following established protocols. These protocols are in effect for security reasons, but they also make it more difficult for authorized individuals to abuse their authority.

Protocols typically dictate when, where, and how records are stored and viewed. For example, a confidential record involving a sexual harassment lawsuit might only be accessible Monday through Friday between the hours of 1:00 pm and 5:00 pm. Authorized personnel must sign the record in and out, and it cannot leave the company premises while they possess it. This protocol provides assurance that the document will not be lost or viewed by unauthorized individuals.

Essentially, protocols involve the storage, retrieval, and distribution of records as follows:

Storage

Organizations must have procedures in place that keep records safe from being viewed by the wrong people, stolen, altered, and/or damaged. This might require housing the documents in humidity or temperature controlled environments. It might also require locked doors, cabinets, drawers, and/or safes. Regardless of the condition or security required, there needs to be a protocol in place for proper storage.

One of the best protocols for storing records involves keeping them offsite in a cloud. This is easy for electronic records, but it requires the scanning of paper documents. Scanning takes time and effort, but it can be a lifesaver if a needed document is missing, altered, damaged, or destroyed.

Retrieval

Once records have been properly stored, procedures need to be in place to retrieve them. These procedures must eliminate the potential for misplacing or losing records once they have been stored. Misplaced paper records can be a nightmare to find, especially as the number of records being stored increases. Electronic records can usually be located with a few clicks of a mouse or a global search, but these records can mistakenly be deleted...and then they are gone permanently if there is no backup.

One procedure for paper record retrieval is a dual sign off sheet. Any record that is retrieved must have two different employee signatures showing that it was retrieved and restored to its designated location. This prevents many of the problems associated with documents being stored in the wrong place.

Electronic records can have a procedure in place that limits their retrieval status to read-only documents. This means they cannot be altered or deleted due to mistakes or purposeful actions.

Distribution

These protocols are similar to those in the section on establishing authority because they designate people who are authorized to see records, but they also establish tracking systems for records once they are circulated. Paper documents can be barcoded to track their movement using scanners. Electronic records, however, are a different story because their movement often cannot be tracked. Someone can post them on the internet or email them to another person...and there is no telling where they will surface again. Since the distribution of electronic records cannot be reliably tracked, the best defense is to store them so they cannot be downloaded, copied, or attached.

Defining life cycles

How long are records stored? Some records are permanent, such as acquisitions or mergers of organizations, because they might need to be referenced at any point in time. Other records might only be kept until a project has concluded, such as the contract for an advertising campaign conducted several years ago. Last, but certainly not least, some records are kept for a specific period of time so they can be reviewed by regulatory agencies, such as credit card receipts for a retail store. The point here is that regardless of the actual time required, every record has a life cycle that needs to be predetermined.

Once a life cycle has concluded, the affected records are typically disposed of so they can no longer be viewed by everyone. However, this raises a question. Can these records be thrown in the trash? The answer is that it depends on the record. Some can be trashed while others need to be destroyed. In fact, the destruction of certain records is so important that it has to be documented...typically by incineration, pulverizing, or shredding. Proof of how they were destroyed and who destroyed them must be available for review by the proper authorities. Examples include human resource records that contain confidential employee information such as names, addresses, birth dates, bank accounts, and social security numbers.

An interesting fact about records that deserves mention is the fact they are not always destroyed after their life cycle. Some organizations archive records that they deem important just in case they are ever needed in the future. For example, a company might keep all financial statement regardless of their age. These records do not require storage, but somebody might want to get a snapshot of the company's financial health at some point in the past. Additionally, records with some type of historical value might be stored or displayed in museums or collections maintained by individuals, clubs, groups, or societies. An example of this is a contract signed by the members of a rock-n-roll band before they were famous.

Electronic vs. paper

This is one of the biggest challenges of record keeping today, and that is why it deserves to be discussed as an aspect of records management. Electronic records have simplified things in many ways, from creation to destruction, but they have shortfalls in terms of authenticity and security. It is easy for many different people to change information on these documents, and they cannot realistically be protected from getting into the hands of unauthorized individuals. Because of this, organizations are working on better ways to store, protect, and retrieve electronic records...but these processes are not foolproof.

Many organizations use paper and electronic records, with the goal being to eventually make everything electronic. This appears to be the way of the future because there are so many positives associated with electronic records. However, electronic records are always the right choice because there are some downfalls associated with them. Some of the major pros and cons are listed below:

Pros

Cost - Cost is one of the biggest advantages of electronic records. They are much cheaper than paper records, and the cost to produce and store digital data continues to go down. If money was the only concern, then electronic records would always be the best choice.

Retrieving – It is relatively easy to retrieve an electronic document. If it is lost, a simple "global search" can usually track it down. Paper documents that are lost or misfiled run the risk of never being found...especially if many different files are involved.

Sharing – Electronic files are easy to share with others. Copies are not necessary and nothing needs to be mailed, faxed, or physically transported to the recipient. A few simple clicks of a mouse and the record can be viewed by others.

Space – Electronic records take up far less space than those made of paper. A hard drive or offsite cloud is capable of holding more records than an entire room of the same paper documents. This is a huge benefit for companies that have limited space to conduct business.

Time – Paper records take time to label, file, manage, and retrieve...much more time than is needed for electronic records. Time is money, and it is a major reason why organizations charge customers a fee to send paper rather than electronic files. Again, if money was the only concern, electronic records would always be the first choice.

Cons

Tracking – It can be difficult to track electronic records because they cannot reliably be scanned. This is in sharp contrast to paper records, which are easily barcoded and traceable wherever they travel. Over time, the electronic tracking problem will likely cease to exist, but it is presently an issue.

Security – Every type of electronic record can potentially be hijacked or rendered useless by hackers or viruses. It is also difficult to prevent electronic records from being sent to unauthorized individuals. Some records can be sent off by simply attaching them to an email…which requires no special technical skills. For these reasons, security is a major negative for electronic records.

Formatting – Records saved in one format cannot always be opened in another format. When this happens, someone who needs the record might not be able to view it. This is very frustrating, and it can be expensive if the records need to be reformatted in order to be viewed

Deleting – This is potentially the biggest disadvantage of electronic records. With a few clicks of a mouse, a digital document can be lost forever. Many companies backup electronic records offsite or on a cloud, but those without a backup plan can permanently do permanent damage.

Based on what has been written in this book so far, it is clear that record keeping is not a simple process. It involves more than filing every document generated. Decisions need to be made and protocols must be in place from record creation to record destruction. This leads us to the next section that discusses the major reasons why records are generated and retained by organizations.

Reasons

Why do organizations maintain records? This is a question with many different answers because records are not all kept for the same reasons. Some records are preserved for fun or entertainment purposes. For example, the *Guinness Book of World Records* contains many different records that do little other than entertain. Other records are held to denote achievements, such as the most strikeouts by a Major League Baseball pitcher.

In organizations, certain records might be held for entertainment and achievement purposes, but the majority of them are kept for legality, ethics, trends, history, and reference reasons. Each of these reasons is described below for easy understanding.

Legality

In many instances, this is the most important reason for keeping records. Records needed during litigation can save organizations time and money, and they might even prevent jail time for employees accused of breaking the law. For example, records from travel expense records can show that an employee was not present when a wrongful activity took place, so she could not have taken part in it. Along the same lines, a laboratory analysis record can show that a manufacturer was in compliance with state or local pollutant regulations.

Records are also kept to avoid different types of legal action. They are especially useful for employee terminations because workers who believe they were wrongfully terminated often go through the court system to get compensated for their loss. For example, records might show that an employee was given written warnings and suspensions before being terminated for actions that violate company policies. This documentation prevents attorneys from taking the employee on as a client because they know they will likely not win the case.

Last, but certainly not least, records are maintained for legal purposes involving confidentially. Some business transactions are not allowed to be released for privacy purposes, but they need to be retained to prove the activity took place. An example is a payment to an employee who sued a management member for sexual harassment. The employee and/or company might not want this information to become public, but they need documentation of the payout to avoid further legal action.

Ethics

Records are often used to prove organizations are doing what is expected of them in order to get something in return. For example, if financial records indicate that a company is very profitable, then they can use those records to obtain bank loans for expansion. However, records are also maintained to show acts of good faith that are not needed for legal, financial, or historical reasons. For example, records might show that a computer manufacturer goes above and beyond the law for recycling of their waste. These records make the company look good in the eyes of environmentalists because the ethical actions were not mandated by law. Along the same lines, a neighboring auto parts distributor might have records showing that they never exceed the absolute minimum legal requirements for recycling waste. While their actions are not illegal, they might be termed unethical by environmental watch groups.

Ethics-related records are becoming more important as people all over the world demand higher standards. Gone are the days when organizations could sweep their unethical activities "under the rug" and maintain the same status quo. For this reason, documents detailing ethical behavior might become some of the most important records in the future.

Trends

Records are great for discovering and tracking trends in organizations. In sales, for example, they show sales of individual products, peak sales periods, and increases or decreases in sales volume compared to the same time period in past years. This information allows companies to make decisions about the products or services they can offer their customers, the inventory that needs to be kept on hand, and the demand that needs to be met at any given time period.

Trends are important for virtually every aspect of business, not just sales, and they can usually be spotted using records from the present and past. Records show employee injuries, raw material changes, consumer preferences, profitability, order history, inventory costs, employee demographics, and a wide variety of other different things. It can safely be said that trends play a huge role in evaluating happenings within organizations, and records provide the most viable and time-saving way to track them.

History

Historical records are often the most popular because they are interesting to peruse. People enjoy reading about the history organizations that they like or patronize. They want to know when the company started, why it started, who founded it, and what was involved at the time of conception. This paints a clear picture of the company and its reason for becoming a business. Once this image is established, it usually remains in the minds of people and influences their thinking.

Although usually not required, leaders tend to keep historical records because they help create positive perceptions of their companies. When people like historical records, they form a subconscious bond with the organization that generates them. They identify with the reasons for the company's being, and this makes them more likely to purchase its products and services. Essentially, historical records are a great sales tool when properly utilized and savvy marketers take full advantage of this potential.

Reference

Records are a great reference for all sorts of different information. For example, a company might want to see the cost of employee benefit packages for the past 20 years. This reason overlaps a bit with history and trends, but it also addresses areas that involve processes and procedures. For example, a policy record might indicate that hourly employees must not punch in more than ten minutes before their start time to avoid extra hours being added by the time clock. Another example is a process that needs to be followed in order to make a piece of furniture the same every time. Processes and procedures provide structure, prevent chaos, and improve efficiency in workplaces, and records are created so those processes and procedures are available for review.

Summary

Record keeping is more important now that it has ever been in the past because records provide valuable resources for preventing lawsuits, providing documentation, indicating peaks, promoting images, and signifying consistency. They prove businesses comply with established requirements, note their positive efforts, and improve their credibility in the eyes of shareholders, government agencies, consumers, and/or the public.

This book examines record keeping in organizations. It designates record classifications, defines management responsibilities, establishes authorized reviewers, discusses security protocols, denotes life cycles, and points out the differences between electronic and paper documents. It also shows how records are critical for legal issues, ethical concerns, trend tracking, historical purposes, and reference reasons.

Congratulations! You now understand more about record keeping in organizations....an increasingly significant aspect of every business.

Employee Reviews
The Appraisal Process and Methods for Improvement

Louis Bevoc

Published by
NutriNiche System LLC

Louis Bevoc books...simple explanations of complex subjects

Introduction	62
Types	62
Supervisor	62
Self	63
Peer	63
360	64
MBO	65
Scale	65
Challenges	66
Supervisor	66
Self	67
Peer	67
360	67
MBO	67
Scale	68
Improving	68
Supervisor	69
Self	70
Peer	71
360	72
MBO	72
Scale	73
Summary	73

Introduction

Leaders of organizations must be able to determine if employees are meeting workplace expectations, and this is best done by using some type of review system that measures their performance. Performance involves standards, levels, or grades that need to be met or exceeded for a particular job or position. Sometimes this can be quantified, like reaching certain numbers for sales or production, but other times it is a bit more complex. For example, it's hard to quantify requirements for research scientists because they typically do not have quotas that need to be achieved. Performance for these individuals might best be measured by the progress and application of their studies and findings.

Without reviews, employees would be somewhat lost. They would not know if they are meeting workplace expectations, and they would find it difficult to achieve organizational goals and objectives. The review process indicates good standing of employees and allows them to monitor their progress as they grow within the organization. Once reviews are complete, employee strengths and weaknesses can be determined and plans for improvement can be implemented if necessary.

This book focuses on specific types of employee reviews, the challenges involved with them, and the best ways for improving them. The types of reviews discussed include *Supervisor, Self, Peer, 360, MBO,* and *Scale*. Each type is analyzed and applied to organizations using workplace examples for better understanding.

Let's begin by discussing the various types of reviews that are used in organizations.

Types

Employee reviews need to be categorized for a better understanding of their importance in the workplace. The following are specific types of reviews that occur in organizations:

Supervisor

This type of review typically involves a one-on-one encounter with the supervisor and employee. The supervisor completes a written evaluation with questions related to performance, including strengths and weaknesses, and discusses it with the employee. The employee has the right to challenge any of aspect of the supervisor's evaluation, and disputes that cannot be resolved are taken to a higher level of management. Once the review is agreed upon by both parties, it becomes a permanent part of the employee's file.

The major advantage of the supervisor review is efficiency. Supervisors typically understand the job responsibilities and expectations of their subordinates. Their familiarity allows them to easily answer most of the review questions, and they are able to make a fairly accurate assessment of employee performance in a reasonable amount of time.

Organizational example

Scott is the production manager in a juice manufacturing plant. He reports to the plant manager Jennifer, and today is his annual review.

Jennifer understands Scott's job responsibilities well because she was the production manager prior to being promoted to plant manager. She thinks he does a good job professionally and also likes him personally. Scott also just finished a project for her that was very successful.

Jennifer answers the review questions on the designated form with no difficulty and then meets with Scott to discuss the details of her evaluation. Scott believes the review is fair and accurate, and it becomes a part of his permanent employee file. This review is simple to conduct and takes less than one hour to complete.

In short, Jennifer understands Scott's job quite well and likes him on a personal and professional level. This allows her to accurately appraise him in a short period of time.

Self

Self-reviews involve employees rating themselves on pre-designated criteria established by the organization. Employees identify their strengths and weaknesses in a variety of areas including performance and work relationships, and they suggest areas where they can improve and grow professionally.

This evaluation can be done using essay responses or a Likert scale. Essays provide a detailed account of employee perceptions, while Likert scales have a range, for instance from 1 to 5, that gives a quantifiable score.

An advantage of self-reviews is that employees gain awareness of their actions and their relationships with others, and this leads to increased accountability.

Organizational example

Ralph works as a bartender at a restaurant that is part of a national chain. He has his six-month review scheduled for today, and corporate management has just informed him that he needs to do a self-evaluation for this appraisal.

Ralph evaluates himself using a Likert scale provided by the company. He rates himself between 1 (poor) and 10 (excellent) for the 20 different categories that assess his performance, growth, and work relationships.

Ralph's scores indicate he has a good relationship with his immediate supervisor, but he needs to improve in three different areas. Because he found the areas for improvement on his own, he is motivated to take accountability and make the necessary changes. These changes should come fairly easy due to the positive association he has with his manager.

Peer

Peer reviews are conducted by team members or coworkers, rather than by the employees themselves or their supervisors. Specifically, peers are asked to anonymously rate the performance of their coworkers. These comments are usually given the supervisor of the employee being reviewed, but sometimes they are also shared directly with the employee. An advantage of peer reviews is that they are often perceived as more fair than reviews conducted by a supervisor because multiple minds provide a more accurate judgment of performance. Additionally, peer reviews are valuable to the workplace in general because they create a culture that encourages feedback and teamwork.

Organizational example

William works as a teller at a bank. His review is scheduled for today, and it will be conducted by his peers. Seven other tellers have shared their opinions about William's performance with Joan, the bank manager.

Joan gathers the information and finds that William is well liked by employees and customers, but he has trouble arriving at work on time. Joan was not aware of this because William starts earlier than her, but she makes sure she shares this information with him.

William is happy that others perceive him as an excellent customer service person. However, he also realizes that his tardiness is an issue because everyone sees it as an area where he needs to improve. Based on his coworkers' analysis, William begins to leave his home earlier in the morning to make sure he arrives to work on time.

In summary, William perceived his peers' critique as fair and legitimate because other tellers had similar comments regarding his performance.

360

This review uses self-analysis, peer assessment, supervisor feedback, and subordinate evaluation (if applicable) for the appraisal. It assesses self-perception (from employees being reviewed), performance (from supervisors), character (from peers), and leadership skills (from subordinates).

The major advantage of the 360 review is that it gives a complete picture of employee performance based on input from multiple sources.

Organizational example

Wanda is a supervisor at an automotive supplier. Her review is today, and her company has decided to a 360 appraisal. The Human resources manager meets with Wanda, her boss, three other supervisors, and three of her direct reports. The appraisal process takes place over the next three days, and the various evaluations do a wonderful job portraying Wanda's performance. Without the input of these different employees, the review would not have as detailed or complete.

In short, Wanda's job performance was clearly depicted due to the diversity of the employees who participated in her evaluation

MBO

MBO is an acronym for "Management By Objectives" that was first popularized in 1954 by management guru Peter Drucker. It involves employees and supervisors working together to establish goals that need to be achieved in a certain time frame. The thinking behind this type of appraisal is that employees who are involved in setting their own goals will be more motivated to accomplish them.

The advantage of MBO reviews is that it is easy to establish success or failure at the next review. Employees are successful if the goals have been achieved, and they have failed if the goals have not been achieved.

Organizational example

Katrina is a sales representative for a line of cosmetics, and her boss Patrick decides to do an MBO evaluation at her mid-year review. Patrick asks Katrina what goals she would like to set for herself. She knows she needs to sell $400,000 worth of product to get a bonus, but she wants to do better. She sets a goal of $500,000 in sales, and Patrick agrees.

For the next six months, Katrina works very hard. She wants to achieve her goal because she established it, and this makes her feel more personally involved. At her year-end review, she achieves her goal of $500,000 in sales, and Patrick rewards her with a raise in her base pay.

In summary, Katrina's involvement in setting a work related goal during her mid-year review motivated her to achieve that goal. By her year-end review, she achieved the goal she established for herself, and Patrick rewarded her for being successful.

Scale

This is a less popular type of review than most of the others because the management has to speed time and effort developing the questions and rating scale that will be used. Essentially, it is a grading system that assesses a variety of aspects related to employee performance including job skills, communication, collaboration, and understanding. Employees need to meet a minimum score, similar to that in education, in order for their review to be considered successful. Those who do not meet the minimum score are put on a performance improvement plan.

The advantage of scale reviews is they are custom made for organizations. This gives management the ability to ask questions that are specific to a particular workplace.

Organizational example

John is a salesperson at a mortgage company, and his review is being conducted using the scale method. John has sold the second most mortgages in the company, proving that he understands his job and is productive. He is also well liked by employees and customers and works well with others on team projects. John easily meets the minimum performance score, and this means that he is successful as a salesperson.

John's job skills, communication, collaboration, and understanding help him achieve a very good score in his review, and this indicates that he is competent in his position.

You now understand some specific types of reviews and the benefits they provide. However, those benefits are sometimes overshadowed by the limitations involved, and that is why the next section is dedicated to the challenges facing the various appraisal processes.

Challenges

As noted above, reviews provide a lot of useful information for employees and managers. However, they are not without challenges, and some of those challenges are discussed in this section.

To make these challenges easier to understand, the same examples from the *Types* section will be used for this section. This time, however, they will be changed to show how the review being discussed has limitations.

Please consider the following:

Supervisor

Supervisor reviews are efficient because bosses typically understand their subordinates job responsibilities and expectations. However, problems with the type of appraisal do exist, and they revolve around bias or slanted thinking.

One issue is the fact these reviews are subjective. A yearly review by a supervisor might be based on the employee's most recent performance, and that performance might not accurately reflect the entire year.

Another concern is the reviews are based on the opinion of one individual. That opinion might not be accurate, and it typically goes unchallenged by anyone else with the authority to make a judgment.

In both situations, the appraisal is not only unfair to the employee being evaluated, it is also unjust for the organizational because they are receiving inaccurate information.

Organizational example

In the *Types* section example, Jenny liked Scott personally and professionally, and this made the review easy for her. However, Scott just finished a big project that was very successful, and that success was in Jenny's recent memory. It caused her to forget about the performance issues Scott experienced at the beginning of the year.

In reality, Jenny's review was unjust to Scott and the juice manufacturer because the documented information was not entirely accurate.

Self

Self-evaluations help employees become aware of the areas they need to improve and motivate them to be accountable. However, this only works if employees are honest with their evaluation....and this is not always the case. For instance, employees might avoid negative supervisor ratings for fear of retaliation or some other undesired outcome.

Organizational example

In the *Types* section example, Ralph evaluated himself and determined that he had a great working relationship with his supervisor. This relationship, however, may be good because his boss is very easy on him. Ralph might be able to do whatever he wants at work with little supervisor intervention, and he does not want this to change based on a critical rating.

Peer

Peer reviews are often perceived as fair because they are conducted by more than one person. This provides a more accurate judgment of the employee being evaluated because more people's opinions are involved. However, a disadvantage of this type of review is peers tend to evaluate coworkers from a personal, rather than professional, level. If they don't like the person, it will reflect their rating in a negative manner.

Organizational example

In the *Types* section example, William found his peers' critiques helpful and legitimate. However, William is well liked by the other tellers. If they did not like him, this would stand in the way of a positive evaluation...regardless of the fact he works well with customers. The end result would be an inaccurate evaluation that casts a negative light on William.

360

The 360 review is very comprehensive because it involves the viewpoints of many different people. However, meeting with all these people is expensive and time consuming. It requires money and time that some organizations simply do not have.

Organizational example

In the *Types* section example, Wanda's appraisal was detailed and complete due to the variety of people involved. However, it required taking seven people away from their jobs for interviews, and it took three days to complete. In short, the 360 review requires valuable resources that many organizations cannot or will not sacrifice.

MBO

The major advantage of MBO reviews is that it is easy to determine success or failure at the next review. Employees are successful if the established goals have been achieved, and they have failed if the established goals have not been achieved. However, employees who fail might lose the motivation and desire to try again…and this is bad for employees and organizations.

Organizational example

In the *Types* section example, Katrina set a goal at her mid-year review and achieved it by her year-end review. Because she was successful, she was rewarded with a raise in her base pay.

If Katrina had not met her goal, her year-end review would have been considerably different. She would not have received the raise, and she would be demotivated by her lack of success. The organization would also suffer because Katrina's failure might deter her from trying again, and she might start looking for other employment.

Scale

Scale reviews are custom made so they allow management the ability to ask questions regarding job skills, communication, collaboration, and understanding that are specific to a particular workplace. However, certain questions can work against introverted individuals. Some people choose their career because it allows them to work independently. They prefer not to socialize or collaborate and typically do not need to do so during their daily activities.

Organizational example

In the *Types* section example, John proved to be competent in his position as a salesperson. He easily met the minimum performance score because he was productive and worked well with others.

The scale review, however, does not give a fair evaluation of other employees at the mortgage company. Marlene is an accountant who rarely needs to interact with people. She is very good at her job, and most of her communication can be done using email. She is an introvert, prefers to work alone, and chose her career based on her work preferences.

Marlene might not achieve the minimum score to be considered successful using the scale system. She is very competent in her position, but her communication and collaboration rating might indicate otherwise. If this is the case, she would need to follow a performance improvement plan, and that would be demotivating for her.

Regardless of the challenges involved with appraisals, they are a necessary part of organizations and will continue to be used until something better comes along. That being said, there must be ways to make them better…and that is the focus of the next section.

Improving

Since there are obvious challenges involved with reviews, it makes sense that they should try to be improved upon. This section examines ways to make reviews better.

To make these methods simpler to comprehend, we will use the same examples from the *Types and Challenges* sections. This time, however, they will be modified to show how the review being discussed can be improved.

Please consider the following:

Supervisor

Supervisor reviews have the advantage of being efficient because bosses are familiar with their subordinate's job responsibilities, and they can make an assessment in a relatively short period of time. However, these reviews are very subjective and can be biased. Additionally, they might be based on the most recent performance of employees, rather than the entire time period for which they are being reviewed.

Ways to improve supervisor reviews include:

Implement training

Supervisors need to be properly trained in order to give meaningful reviews. This training will teach them how to provide positive and negative feedback in a way that helps employees become successful and achieve organizational objectives. This is best done in face-to-face meetings, but web-based resources and tools can be provided for reference at any time.

Monitor appraisals

Supervisor appraisals need to be monitored after they are completed due to the subjectivity and potential bias involved. This is best done by someone in upper management who makes sure the evaluation is accurate and the employee and organization are being treated fairly.

Utilize other supervisors

Supervisors should meet with each to discuss the review process. This collaboration encourages learning, promotes best practices, and creates consistency of appraisals throughout the organization.

Organizational example

In the *Types* and *Challenges* section example, Scott just finished a big project that was very successful, and that success caused Jenny to forget about the performance issues he had at the beginning of the year. Due to this, her review of him was inaccurate.

The inaccuracy in this review could have been avoided if Jenny was properly trained. She could have been taught how to reflect on the entire year and provide difficult feedback to help Scott improve in the areas that he is weak.

Additionally, Jenny's appraisal should have been reviewed by someone in higher management. This monitoring would have discovered that Jenny did not note any negative aspects of Scott's performance. She could then have been instructed to go through training in order to perform reviews that are best for the employee and the company.

Self

The advantage of self-reviews is that employees gain awareness by identifying their strengths and weaknesses, and this leads to increased accountability. However, this evaluation only works if the employees are truthful about their perceptions. Dishonestly is common during self-appraisals due to fear of retaliation and other negative outcomes.

The best way to improve self-reviews is to get upper management involved. They can hold meetings to encourage truthful and meaningful thinking that promotes accurate self-evaluations. Specifically, the goals of these meetings are to:

Encourage self-promotion

Employees who believe they are doing well in certain areas need to be able to express this without being thought of as bragging. Accomplishments and successes must be noted for recognition and rewards, and this starts with the persuasion of upper management.

Encourage constructive criticism

Employees who have negative feelings about supervisors must be able to express them without fear of those supervisors retaliating. The best protection from this retaliation comes from managers at the top, and they need to communicate their intent to supervisors and employees.

Encourage objectivity

Employees who know they need to improve in certain areas must realize their weaknesses and seek to get better. Employees who are not objective risk losing an opportunity to grow and progress within the organization...and leadership needs to make this clear.

Encourage requests for guidance

Employees who face challenges must feel comfortable asking for help in the form of training, teaching, or mentoring. They also need to know that they will receive assistance when they ask for it, and upper management can provide that assistance.

Encourage planning

Employees need confidence to plan for their future. They need to know where they are and where they want to go, and this is made possible with the support of organizational leadership.

In short, improvement of self-reviews stems from top management guiding employees, holding them accountable, protecting them, and making them aware that self-appraisals are part of a learning process that benefits their professional growth.

Organizational example

In the *Types* and *Challenges* section example, Ralph was objective in his self-review because he found areas where he needed to improve. He also determined that he had a good working relationship with his supervisor, but this might have been because his boss was very easy on him.

If Ralph is doing whatever he wants to do with little supervision, then he is not progressing or learning...and this could have been pointed out to him by company leaders. Meetings with management could have made it clear that he needed to find some constructive criticism about his boss for the review to be truly beneficial.

Peer

The advantage of peer reviews is that they are perceived as fair by employees because the evaluation comes from several people rather than one supervisor. However, peers tend to evaluate each other based on personal, rather than professional, relationships.

Personal relationships at work are important, but they do not accurately represent job performance. Some employees are very good at their jobs, but they are not well liked by others. Other employees are well liked by coworkers, but they are not very good at their jobs.

Since peer reviews are often based on personal relationships, the best way to improve them is to avoid using them for monetary compensation, promotions, or disciplinary action. Instead, they should be used as reference tools to help upper management make decisions related to these three areas.

Organizational example

In the *Types* and *Challenges* section example, William was well liked by others. Due to this, he was rated as an excellent customer service person. If he was not well liked, his rating likely would have been much lower. In either case, the rating would be somewhat inaccurate because it is based on personal likes and dislikes rather than performance.

Although Williams review was based mostly on personal relationships, it did have value. It made him realize that he needs to get to work earlier to avoid being late. It also encouraged collaboration among his peers, and this helps improve the overall communication at the bank.

Williams rating, however, should not be used to determine his pay, bonus, or potential for promotion. It should be used by bank executives, along with other tools such as his supervisor's review, to establish these important job aspects.

360

The 360 review is advantageous because it uses multiple sources (self, coworkers, higher management, and subordinates) at a variety of hierarchy levels for the evaluation. However, this appraisal is also time consuming and costly, so it is not feasible for some organizations.

Planning and commitment are important for improving the 360 review. Planning involves making sure the proper resources, time and money, are available from start to finish. Top management also needs to be committed to being part of the process, rather than spectators on the sidelines.

Organizational example

In the *Types* and *Challenges* section example, Wanda's review involved seven people and took three days to complete. Her appraisal was detailed and complete, but three days is a long time for an evaluation. Better planning should have been made in advance to make sure the employees being interviewed for the assessment were ready at the designated times. This would have saved time that could have been better used in those employees' daily jobs. Additionally, a person in an executive position at the automotive supplier should have been present during the interviews. Although this might seem like additional resources being utilized, executives see important areas of evaluations that need to be addressed, and they help expedite the overall process.

MBO

The advantage of MBO reviews is they make it simple to establish success and failure. If objectives have been achieved, then the employee is successful. If objectives have not been achieved, then the employee has failed.

A clear distinction between success and failure is good for those who succeed, but it is not good for those who fail. In fact, those who fail might not be motivated to try again, and this is bad for the employee and the organization.

MBO appraisals can be improved by providing adequate time and training. Employees and supervisors need to be properly trained in order to understand how to set realistic objectives that are achievable...and this takes time.

Organizational example

In the *Types* and *Challenges* section example, Katrina was successful because she accomplished her objectives. However, she might not be successful in her next review, and this could discourage her from trying again. If Katrina undergoes training on how to set realistic objectives, then she could avoid the failure of not reaching her objectives. This requires time, but the payback will be worth it because Katrina's continual success is important for helping the company thrive and prosper. In other words, Katrina's success is directly related to the success of the organization.

Scale

Scale reviews have an advantage over other types of evaluations because organizations can design them to fit specific needs. However, these appraisals are not good for employees who are introverted or work independently.

Scale reviews can be improved by eliminating or modifying some of the questions that evaluate communication and collaboration for certain individuals. In other words, the evaluation will change based on the personality and/or position of the employee.

Organizational example

In the *Types* and *Challenges* section example, John did quite well on the scale appraisal because he is an extroverted salesperson. The same review, however, is not fair to Marlene because she is an introverted accountant. Management needs to take this discrepancy into account and alter some of the communication and collaboration questions for Marlene so she gets an accurate review and avoids being put on a demotivating performance improvement plan.

Summary

Employee reviews are an important aspect of most organizations because they evaluate an individual's performance. They indicate a worker's strengths and weaknesses, and they play a large role in determining that person's monetary compensation and promotion opportunities. Without reviews, employees would not know if they are progressing at their jobs, and they would not understand their job expectations.

This book uses thoughtful analysis and workplace examples to examine specific types of employee reviews, the challenges involved with them, and the best ways for improving them. The types of reviews discussed include *Supervisor, Self, Peer, 360, MBO,* and *Scale*.

After reading the material in this book, you will have a better understanding of reviews and their importance in the workplace.

www.ingramcontent.com/pod-product-compliance
Lightning Source LLC
Chambersburg PA
CBHW030455220526
45464CB00006B/2547